Sofia Grosch

Ocean Pearl

Impressum

1. Auflage 2023

Copyright © 2023 Sofia Grosch

Rathausstraße 51, 68535 Edingen-Neckarhausen

Umschlaggestaltung: Sofia Grosch

Satz: Constanze Kramer, coverboutique.de

Herstellung und Verlag:
BoD – Books on Demand, Norderstedt

ISBN 978-3-73474-535-5

Continents

drowning

you are the ocean
i am lost in
so deep
i think i am drowning

"be strong, be strong, be strong"
until i breakdown
under the pressure
of mantaining a strength i never had
no make up can cover up the sadness in my eyes
every word i try so say
comes out in trembling pain
my heart is no longer shattered
it is completely empty
equals a dark hole
i never thought
that to feel numb
would be worse
than to feel pain.

Sofia Grosch

we think we can escape from everything
if we go far away
but we forget
that we can't escape our minds

it seems
to be
weeks
since we said
goodbye
but it was
this morning
and i can't deny
how afraid i feel
about this upcoming time

to me
you were
an entire ocean

the first time we kissed
i fell in love with you
but i kept falling
now lying on the ground
i can't get back up

Sofia Grosch

you gave me a taste
of how life would have been
with you beside me
ever since i am starving

starving for the love and feelings
you made me feel
eternally wondering why you left
after giving me everything i never had

you left me alone with a hunger
no one can feed

Ocean Pearl

i feel so empty
because you took everything from me
but at the same time i feel full
full of the broken pieces
you left inside of me

one day
i will be okay
when i think about you
about us
and all that we have lost

but right now
i am drowning
in the sea
of heartbreak
sorrounded
by the tears of strangers
and my own
why do i feel so alone
when there are thousands
of others
going through the same
stage of pain

how tragic it is
that we give up on love so easily
instead of giving up the person
that hurt and betrayed us

i don't like
to think of myself
as a fragment
i always wanted
to be whole
on my own
but now
that you are gone
i have lost
most parts of myself
all that is left
is this little piece
of a puzzle
and i don't know
where to start
looking
for the missing pieces

you can change
or stay the same
but do not expect
of me
to stay around any longer
i gave you
enough time
i gave all my
patience to you
i even gave you
my heart
and when i had the courage
to leave
i left with empty hands
with an empty heart
i had nothing left.

you stand there
staring at me
while i am burning down
in flames

Sofia Grosch

it is not possible
to make your wings
grow back
by cutting off
the ones
of your children

its all the times you told me i deserve nothing
that makes me feel guilty when happiness finds it's way
to me
its every night i wanted to talk to you
but you told me to shut
that makes me worry people don't care for what i have
to say
its all the times i tried to impress you
but you wouldn't even look
that still to this day
i need to remind myself
i deserve happiness
i can expect of others to listen to me
and i don't need to impress people
in order for me to feel valuable
i already am worthy and enough
and i have always been

you expected of a child
to be as mature as an adult
no mistakes only perfection was good
but still not good enough for you

we shouldn't have to be
miles apart
to get along

in public you told me to hold your hand
at home all you did
was to push me away from you

– you made me confound affection and aversion at a
very young age

i don't see
how you continue
to abuse
the ones
you claim
to love

communication is the key
a lot of people are missing

don't mistake my kindness
with blindness
i am aware of your actions
but choose to not raise my voice
for my mother taught me
to stay calm and kind
for it's empty minds
that have voices loud as lions
where only noise comes out
but commonsense is left out

they look away when it happens
out of fear they could be next

– bullying

i remember this boy
back in my last year of school
making fun about a girl
for not shaving the hair of her armpits and legs
his laugh and words had me speechless

so it is okay
to point out the body hair of women
but its the most normal thing for men
to have it everywhere
even considered attractive
but on women it causes disgust

let me tell you what's really disgusting
… these kind of stigmas

my body is no invitation
neither is a short dress or skirt
as long as i don't clearly say yes
it is always a no

you have caused
heavy rainfalls
inside of me
internal storms
that damaged me

when you told me
i had become
a bad habit of yours
i wanted to cry
instead
i have kissed you
as strong and long
as possible
i knew
it would be the very last time
i would ever feel your lips
on mine

the way he made you feel
so special and beautiful
was nothing more
than cheap lies

insane how good an actor you are

if only you had looked closer at her
you could have seen who she really was
she had so much more to offer
than her beauty
her eyes told stories
filled with wisdom
she learned from the lessons of life
something raw and wild in the way she saw this world
and even wilder the way she looked at you
but you only liked her for the way she looked
so you could stare at her for hours
and still not see her

how did we end up here
and why didn't i see it coming

– my head hurts from overthinking

to know you
is both
a blessing and a curse
it was the beginning of my art
but the end of me

my healed scars
start bleeding
when i see you

trying to escape you
is running through a labyrinth
with no exit

please let me breath
i gave you a place to live
i gave all of me to you
why are you taking away my life

– earth

the first kiss after the breakup
was an explosion of emotions
with the taste of desperation on your tongue

– second chance

he kissed my opinion away

– i should have seen the signs

there are times
where i question
my whole existence
i keep asking myself
if there is anything
i can be good at
or if i am just good at failing
but i now know
that these times
also pass
they are not the end of me
just a part of me

– depression

winter came by fast
in my opinion too fast
still so many things on my list that i wanted to do with
you
but now you are distant and turned cold
to busy to spend time with me
now all i have are the memories
of a summer i hope i never forget
wild and beautiful
yet so short
day and night we had spend awake living and loving
as if there was no tomorrow
as if a part of us had already known
that by the time summer would end
our lovestory would have too

no sunset will bring you back

still
i run down to the beach
every evening
when the sun starts setting
i wait patiently
in hopes you might come back
i wait till the sky
turns into dark blue
then i go back to the house
thinking of you

and the pain in my heart
becomes less present
as time keeps passing
but when it is present
i still feel nine years old
i start to feel unsafe
in a safe place
my mind shifts back into a state of mind
i always wanted to escape
everytime it comes back
i become the victim i once was

– flashbacks

i fell into oblivion
my heart could no longer
bare the stress

although there are millions of roads
there is not one that leads me back to you

i was at the edge
of giving up
when you came
and hugged me from behind
you showed me life
through your eyes
and gave me a new perspective
you made me feel
seen and loved
you have listened
i felt understood for the very first time
and that was what made my hope
come back to life

out of the ocean

my lungs are filled with water
my eyes are burning from the salt
trembling i am crawling out of the ocean
in need of oxygen

there are times when we bloom
and times when we fall apart
leaving parts of us behind
just as trees lose their leaves
but that is okay
because we will start to bloom again

we can't go back in time
to change our actions
or erase the words we said
what we can change is the present
for a different future

the love a mother has for her children
is the purest thing that exists on earth

i want to get
to a state of mind
where peace is the foundation
of it all
but my head right now
equals a troubled sea
what do i have to do
the moon smiled and answered
it is not about doing anything
it is about time to stop
holding on to everything
your past is over
still you keep carrying it with you
every where you go
you want peace
but cling to your past
as if it is all you have
you are missing out on the present
twenty years from now
you will once again be living in the past
trying to relive
the moments you now let pass
be here now
let go of what is gone
focus on living in the present
and you will feel
a change in your mind

– be here

the moon is my friend
he stays up with me
whenever i can't sleep
he listens and talks back to me
he always makes his light shine
upon my dark thoughts
to make them bright again

believing in myself
was a very brave act
considering
the many years
he tried to make me
hate and doubt myself

vulnerability is my greatest strength

Ocean Pearl

i let my thoughts
out into the ocean
and watch the waves
carry them away

Sofia Grosch

she is one old soul
stuck in this modern world

often my mind feels endless
different universes
different languages
languages i don't understand
universes i want to escape
but i can't get away

not even in my wildest dreams
i would have thought
i once would be your home

you found home
in the most different places
in the mountains
in the ocean
under the sky and in sunrises
but never in a person
to hear you say
you found home in me
is the purest and most beautiful thing
anyone could have told me

as i lay my head on his chest
i start to calm down
the feelings of anxiety
slow down
but then
a thought crosses my mind
what will i do
if one day
he won't be by my side
no chest to rest on
no one to call home
my heart starts running wild
as if i would already be alone
but he is by my side
and my head still rests on his chest

take me away
for a couple of days
i want to escape the black and white
people have forgotten how to love and how to be kind
i want us to start living in colors
we should escape this city
and go to naples
where time stops for a little while
where you are sorrounded by the smell
of the ocean
wandering between colorful houses
where people receive you warmly
without knowing you
for all they know is love
take me away, take me away

nothing feels better
than being loved
by the person
your heart longs for

even
in a museum
it is you
that is the most mesmerizing
piece of art
you are my muse
your eyes are a door
to a soul
i hope
i never have to live without

you read a lot of books, he said

i love reading novels with happy ends

why? he asked

until i can have one for myself i will keep on reading
them, to never lose hope
i answered

i have learned to accept people as they are
when i was not accepted

waves are part of the ocean
just as they are part of life too

words mean nothing
if your actions contradict
what you say

i disconnect from this world
so very often
it has become a rarity
to feel connected to it

we never think twice about breathing
because we know we can't live without oxygen
still when it comes to food and eating
we often think in such cruel ways
starving and punishing ourselves
to look a certain way

in order to grow from pain
we have to confront ourselves with it
no matter how hard it is
we need to understand what is hurting us
to find a solution for it

but dear
you must stop looking for healing
in the people who hurt you

i will be brave and make you proud
– to my nine year old self

tonight the moon is full
and just like the moon
i am whole again
i am no longer
a lesser part of myself
because of you

the word women
becomes more powerful
with every new generation born

Sofia Grosch

how you see yourself
is how others will see you too

if only
you could see
what i see
you have grown
so much
you are blooming
reaching the roof
with your flowers
upholding yourself
in storms
what you have accomplished
is more than
astonishing

everything you need
is within you
believe in your powers

you need to remember
how far you have come
there are oceans between
where you were
and where you are now
regardless of the road
you still have ahead of yourself
i want you to embrace the path you have taken
i want you to embrace yourself

venting is tempting
to remain calm
and rethink the situation
takes the strength
you have

the time will come
where you will be able
to look at your scars
without seeing the battlewounds
that caused them

Sofia Grosch

don't let your pride
hold you back
from accepting help

being kind to others and yourself
brings you peace

the moon
rises every night
no matter how
small or full he is
i hope
you realize
that you too
can shine
no matter
your size or age

how she made
the best
out of the worst
will forever
stay with me

perhabs
these painful times
are a way of life
to make our hearts stronger
not less soft
but maybe give them the strength
to endure pain that is inevitable
to survive and heal again

where do i start
to find myself
to become and be
the person i already
carry inside of me
but never see
hidden under the mask
anorexia made me wear
hidden behind the shadows
of this illness
i feel myself awakening
getting up to start fighting
to get to the front
to replace the eating disorder
with my true self

– becoming

i continue
to gain back
trust in myself
in all my strengths
and i also
continue
to lose all your bitterness
you fed me with

he tried to tame me
and failed
i had already told him
the only one
who can change me
is myself

i won't try
to compete with her
just because
you decide
to compare us
to eachother

some days the only thing left of me
is my shell
in which i crawl
into the smallest corner
i wrap my arms around myself
to hold myself as tight as possible
in case i would fall apart
the second i loosen up my grip
i tell myself it will be okay again
this feeling will pass
you will make it through
you will make it through
you will make it through

– anxiety

i run
to escape the anger and pain
some days
i win the race
other days
i lose

i know
there will be days
when i get
overflowed by the waves
of missing you
i will let them
wash over me
i will sit in them
and cry
but i won't let them make me suffocate.

as ever
my heart
longs for yours
but not everything
we want
is good for us

the distance between us
is not to blame
neither is one of us
with time comes change
and we changed a lot

there are days i feel so close to you
as if there were not thousands of miles
between us
then there are days where the distance couldn't be
bigger
worlds between us
and our hearts don't remember what its like being
together

it is like we are on a ferris wheel
driving laps with highs and lows
yet we don't get any further
we just keep going around in circles

– not meant to be

maybe i should let you go
maybe i should stop sticking to the past
maybe i should stop believing that you are the same
person
as your were back then
for we are all constantly changing
and deep inside me i know
i have to forget you
but maybe i can't

i was convinced
we would be forever
i guess
that was another
lesson of life
i had to learn
nothing is guaranteed

give me time
to unlearn
the destructive
patterns
that have kept me
alive
i am aware
they don't serve me
anymore
but my brain
is not

i tried to explain myself to people
that wouldn't listen
but i couldn't tell
because they were looking at me the whole time

your love and all that you are is so enough
you are more than enough
you are the most wonderful human being
and i wish
i trully wish i could be the right person for you
but i am not
each of our experinces change us
yet there are things that remain
fears and doubts that might stay
you deserve someone who trusts you blindly
a person to love you with all of their heart
someone who isn't afraid of falling in love
you deserve the world
you even gave me the chance to become yours
but i destroyed it
you are the safest person
the safest place to be
and i know it may sound ridiculous
but maybe thats what scared me the most
because i never felt safe before

dear moon
where are you
i miss our long night talks
i miss your voice
i miss your advice
i miss myself

i want to run back
into the ocean
and get lost in it

swimming

deep down in the ocean
under all the big waves
i have found myself a safe place

wake up, he said
you have been dreaming for too long
you should start to make your dreams come true
you are right, i answered
and got up

i am beginning to understand
that nothing is going to change
if i don't leave my comfort zone
i have to dare to do things
even when i am afraid
because if i don't do it
no one will do it for me

after you cut my wings
i tried for the longest time
to make them grow back
but it was when i stopped
focusing on what you had taken
from me
that i realized
i could fly without wings

gratitude over bitterness

after all i still cherish what we had
for it taught me to let go
of what isn't meant to be

you don't owe them
anything
you only owe it
yourself
to fight for the life
you have always dreamed of

you are not a slave of the past
you have survived it
you are destined for more

i aspire to become
as patient with myself
as my mother is with me

what has changed is
when you tell me
i can't do it
i hear
that you can't believe in yourself
and therefore you can't believe in me
neither
but now i believe in myself
and i can believe in you too

how do i take my power back?

– by loving and accepting yourself

i used to take everything people told me very personal
it made me cry a lot
until one day i sat down
thinking for hours
about these people
and i realized
how they talk to others
is how they must talk to themselves
they must be so full of negativity
it even bursts out of their mouth

your attempts
to win me back
with materialistic gifts
show
how little you know me

Sofia Grosch

the world has enough space
for you
to be yourself

my dear body
thank you for all you do
and did to keep me alive
even though the only thing
you got from me in return
these past years
has been hate
i deeply apologize yet i know
no apology could ever mean as much
as starting to embrace and love you
for all you do
and all that you are
with the scars on my arm
and the stretchmarks on my hips
from gaining back life
therefore i will love you so very much
for you always deserved to be loved

embrace your blooming body

the amount of times
you have told me
i wasn't good enough
can no longer compare
with the times
i have told myself
i am enough

– taking back my power

i won't be your victim ever again

your lies run marathons
but keep in mind
that every marathon has an end

Sofia Grosch

i am no longer
worrying about
what could go wrong
for once
i am thinking about
what could work out

just as you have learned to ride the waves
you will learn to climb the mountains

i jump into the unknown
full of joy
full of life

– ready for new beginnings

what does it feel like
to be at peace with yourself and life
i wondered about it for years
until i realized with twenty one years
to achieve that
i had to accept what i couldn't change
i had to stop comparing my journey
to others
i had to learn i can't please everyone
i had to give up all control
i took over myself
instead i decided to trust life
i started to focus on the things i was able to do
i began speaking as kindly to myself
as i did to my friends
i didn't punish myself over little mistakes
i went from being my enemy to a friend
who wants the best for me
slowly i started seeing changes
in myself, my sorroundings and life itself
a new door had opened and the key had been in me
the whole time

nothing you say
will reach me again
only the waves
of the past
but even they
will become less
and softer
as time goes on

and even on the days
where going back
seems more soothing
i remind myself
of the many reasons
i started to fight
to get to live
a normal life

– existing wasn't living

she carried her struggles
with so much grace
no one would have
imagined
the troubles
she had to face

i am creating
the life
i want to live

it was time to leave the past behind

the future starts now

the moment
i realized
only i could decide
how i react
to situations
everything changed

you told me
i would fail
be nothing without you
but now
that i am without you
i am everything
i always wanted to be

– free

Sofia Grosch

i am not longer a victim
the waves have washed away
the marks
your dirty hands left on me
i am not longer drowning
i am swimming
in the deepest part of the ocean
this is just the beginning
of living and becoming
i have found my voice again

when i stopped waiting
for the apology
that would never come
i realized
i didn't need it to move on

he called me smart
before calling me pretty

– the type of men i like

the intimacy
of knowing
each others thoughts
just by looking
into the eyes

our bond is both strong and soft
it doesn't engage
still it could hold us
over the ocean
and from falling down hills

pain
comes and goes
in waves
or heavy rains
happiness
aswell
comes and goes
sometimes
for a short glimpse
and sometimes
for a couple of days

what makes him so special?

"he made me feel special, no one ever did that before."

Ocean Pearl

i can lose myself in you
over and over again
because you will always find me

Sofia Grosch

i let him
unfold
my heart

you made it
easy for me
to learn
to trust again

The funny thing is how i didn't search for you at all.
But when you crashed into my life, it made
perfect sense. It has always been you. You lived in my
imagination before i met you.
From the first day you have been so soft with my heart.
You hold it so gently as if it was made out of porcelain.
I have never felt this safe before.
Loving you is my favourite thing to do. And even
though i don't believe in forever i hope
i get to spend forever with you.

he must be
from a different
galaxy
he is too wonderful
to be from this world

some people will come into your life
when you least expect it
they will change it completely
in a good way
a mesmerizing way
that makes you wonder
what you did
to deserve so much love and goodness
those are the people
that show you
why it was worth it to not give up
people
that make you believe
in love again

our sunday escapes
are my favourite
just the two of us
in a place
we have never seen before
discovering its magic
as we keep
discovering ourselves

although
he is my safe haven
i still am
my own anchor

she is the calm
in the deepest sea

you broke me
but i healed myself

– stronger

everything takes time
some things more
some less
but when it comes
to your health
you should take
all the time you need

Sofia Grosch

she was feeling
the pressure of the world
weighing her down
and for a moment
it was tempting
to try to lift it up herself
but she knew
it would be silly
so instead she rested
and waited for the world
to roll on

be patient with your heart
in this empty space
i know it seems to be
the end of you
but believe me
when i say
it is full of potential
full of space
for you to create and be

the eating disorder has become a visitor
who visits me in times
i struggle
it always says it wants to help me
luckily, i know the eating disorder lies
but during these times
i am not strong enough
to throw it out of my house
the eating disorder sits down on my couch
watches every step i take
it gets too comfortable around my home

sometimes it only stays a few days
which is then a big relief
but there are occasions where it stays over for months
it is draining and tiring
to live with such a bad visitor
i hope one day
when i find myself struggling
and the doorbell rings
to have the courage to refuse to let it come in

Ocean Pearl

i am no longer
afraid of endings
i know
they bring new beginnings

Sofia Grosch

your body is a temple
you get to call home

– take care of your home

they ask me if i gained weight
i am gaining happiness, i answer

Sofia Grosch

i am becoming the woman
i admired as a child
independent, courageous, smart
and strong
oh how hard i have worked
and still am
to become her
i had to break to start all over
to rebuild myself, to rebuild my home
to heal the wounds of the past
to close this door
took the longest time
but it was so necessary
i arrived in the present
with just a little suitcase
full of coping techniques and my favourite books
after four years of existing
i am finally living

turning pain
into art
is her magic power